she who

Collected Poems
1991-2004

Rachael Clyne

other books
by the same author

Cancer: Your Life - Your Choice
Breaking the Spell: the Key to Recovering Self-esteem

she who walks with stones
and sings

Collected Poems
1991-2004

Rachael Clyne

PS AVALON
Glastonbury, England

© Rachael Clyne 2006

First published in the U.K. in 2006 by PS Avalon

PS Avalon
Box 1865, Glastonbury
Somerset, BA6 8YR, U.K.

*Rachael Clyne asserts the moral right
to be identified as the author of this work*

sculpture: Rachael Clyne
photography: Collette Barnard

design: Will Parfitt

All rights reserved. No part of this publication may be reproduced, sorted in a retrieval system, or transmitted in any form or by any means, electronic, mechanical, photocopying, recording or otherwise, without the prior permission of the publisher.

ISBN 0-9544764-6-8

CONTENTS

SENSE OF PLACE AND SEASON

Prayer For The Ancestors	9
Winter Joy	11
Midwinter	12
Imbolc In The Quantocks	13
Migration	14
Cape Cornwall	15
Druid Haven	16
Full Stop	17
Starling Magic	18
Goodbye Coleford	19
Enchanter	20
Gateways	21
Savage Garden	22
Dusk	24

SPIRIT VOICES

She Who Walks With Stones And Sings	27
Hedgewitch	29
Inner Voices	30
Pilgrimage	32
Innana's Journey	34
Signs	36
Proud	38

ARTIST'S EYE

Corners – A Painting Project	41
Blocked	42
Barbara Hepworth's Garden	43

FAMILY PATTERNS

Family Patterns	45
Like Mama Used To Make	46
Absent	47
Last Kaddish	48
Klops	49
Three-Course Meal	50
Animus	52
Magic Suit	54
Release	55
The Golem	56
Glamourseekers	58
Sisters	60
Memoriam	62
Thankful To Trees	64
Round Barrows	65

LOVE POEMS

Invitation	67
Aflame	68
Lady Of the Lake	69
Love Hits	70
Storm In A Teacup	71
Swan Song	72
Hostage	74
Harvest At St Ives	75
Surrender	76

MENDING THE BROKEN SELF

Beneath	79
Need	80
Fences	81
New Year Resolution	82
There Comes A Time	83
Heart Of Darkness	84
Healing	86
Survivor's Sunset	87
The Client	88
No More	90
When Life Feels Blue	92

ALL-SORTS

Threshold	95
Ladies Of A Certain Age	97
Senior Moment	98
Sanction	100
Miriam's Gift	101
Small Wonder	102
The Last Lines	103
Islets Of Langerhan	104
Dirty Beast	105
Full Circle	106

Index of first lines	108

sense of place
and season

Prayer For The Ancestors   2000

You called in whispers
and I came.
I felt your body
in my body
sinewy
joyous
a thousand-fold more alive
than my forgotten flesh
treading through my feet
the land you trod
keeping faith
with intimate knowledge of
ragged robin
nuthatch
stooping alder
and rushing water
close as my womb

In your veins
your wise nerve ends
the power of rock and rain
the kiss of stone and earth
with the acuteness
of a lover
knowing
the moment of bud
of seed
of dying
of midnight
of waiting
of dreaming
far beyond

the stars were not distant to you
your voices reach me
in the shriek of wind

in the sanctity of mud
your eyes show me
the looking
the importance of wren
of spotted orchid

I see you muscle-tight
moving through shadows
and the few broken shards
of your remains
are as potent
as when you huddled
in fogous
on hilltops
carving ditches with antlers
raising circles
to remind us of your wisdom

We thank you for your love
for your long long wait
and we hear your
voices at last
you are with us still
and the love you bear
we thank you.

Winter Joy   2002

Winter joy
a rare bright jewel
shining through tracery of branches
etched against
the certainty of death
each moment becomes
beauty sharp
wonder of
leaf shapes, silhouettes
of small simple things
a shoot
pushing up
through
tilled black earth
cleared of Autumn clutter

Inner space
a warm cave
beckoning
amidst frenzied outer rush
ancestor voices crackle
in flames
rustle
in icy wind
"ssshhhh! ssslow dooowwwn!
we have things to tell
lissssten!
gaze!
let us rest you
in the dark
feed your dreams
till waking time"

Midwinter   1999

On the bone edge
there is only breathing
each breath
one breath
an entire lifetime
in a bleached skull reality
each moment
a breath unto itself
and then another
like delicate vertebrae
laced one upon another
as frost on a window pane

Imbolc In The Quantocks 2004

Walking the brown of Your earth into stiff limbs
rich scent of loam in my nostrils
passing through lichen-cloaked trees,
Your woodland brook
swelled with winter rain
cleanses my heart
water streams from my nose, my eyes
in the chill of the day

Scrambling up steep muddy
leaf-mould slopes
panting until
I pour up and out into
Your sunlight
atop your breast, your belly
all heather and bracken
and oh!
the sea, the sky, the land afar,
far as the horizon
Your breath in my lungs, sharp and clear
Your fiery arrows pierce my sloth
I feel the momentary exhilaration of Your quickening
that glimpse of spring to come
this is one such afternoon!
slipping off my dull winter carapace
each step vitality and joy
descending at last to the rich reward of tea
and Stella's homemade cake
how well You provide for us
how I love the beauty of Your seasons!

Migration   1999

Geese fill a flat sky
in wide threads
insistent cries
ebb and flow
ploughing familiar grooves
celestial song-lines
homeward

Amidst a decaying redbrick propriety
that was once my home
good Victorian values
quietly doze
in geriatric dream

The seafront bracing
as I sit on the proud new municipal wall
legs dangling
I gaze across sandy mudflats
to a distant tide

Wheelchairs are wheeled
as the retired take their daily promenade
hand in hand
in neat polyester car coats
while a thousand geese
pass unnoticeably above

Childhood memories enthralled
at the Autumn spectacle
and the unspoken longing
to be with them
on their wild way

Cape Cornwall 2000

On the path, a man lies buried
nearby the grave of a dog
empty leash
coiled grass snake

A bleak promontory rises
uncompromising death's head
topped by crematoria chimney
memorial to tin plunder

Crossing a narrow rock bridge
Charybdis fumes below
black rock teeth bite into a savage sea
they cast our friend's bones
to wind and wave
here at the edge
where wild meets wild

You sit reluctant
on the threshold
as sinister waves
suck at your soul
unready yet to embrace the stark rage
of other deaths looming

A rowboat, silhouette black
bobs in the distance

Yet there is healing here
embracing the edge
where wild meets wild

Druid Haven 2003

Great swathes of slate arch
from the gathering waters
and craggy Welsh grandmother guardians
knap-headed with gorse
heavy-bosomed, tender-hearted
stare out to sea

And there's the walking-windswept sea
the joyous-swimming sea
the crashing cliff-top, rocks-below sea
and the floating mysterious other-world sea

But most of all
there's the shining full-moon-pathway sea
shifting oceans of cloud above as below
melting inlets and strange creatures
archipelagos of light and shadow
glide past her gentle face
casting veils of Spanish lace
upon her radiant smile
and we glow

Full Stop   1994

It takes something the size of a mountain
so huge in stillness
sheep crawl
white flea specks on its back
and tumbling waterfalls
glistening snail-trails
ooze lazily down
to quell my frantic mind

Gazing at mountains
I come to a full stop
myself revealed

Starling Magic   2004

A heron's steady gaze
waits on breakfast
the flat green meadow
sodden dull and magical
spreads to a line of withies
red with rain

A parable of swans graze
in corps de ballet formation

At once
a swoop of starlings
a hundred thousand
slice through the stupor
with sculptural grace
pulling gasps of wonder
from our lips

Twisting dives
and complex spins
adjusting to currents
to each familial other

Spatial perfection
trace subtle lines of air
above the rhyne

No sooner here than gone
with a masterly flourish of wings
a disappearing tide
above clumps of willow

The sky's flesh so vividly drawn
returns to a somnolent posture
moist and hanging
and we leave.

Goodbye Coleford   1996

Swallows perch on telegraph wires
like notes on a bar
a brown man waves
among nodding buttercups
in the water meadow
our tribe around him
ghosts of tomorrow
ice age thaws once more the heart
still wedded through millennia
only this morning
the brush of his megalith lips on mine
hot hair-skin body against me
rock-strong tenderness

this memory fragment
cracks me into ice-floes so deep
my legs fold in the grass
and wrench tears to scald the ragged robin earth

"it's time to let you go" they whisper
as the tribe gathers me
I walk on staff in hand
as I may have done before
to my next destination
will I see you again dear friend o will I?
tomorrow begs the question
as I walk up the lane into today
my car waits while swallows chirrup
notes on a bar
my farewell serenade.

Enchanter At Mells Irish Folk Festival   1994

He raised the bone slivers to scoop up my soul
with a lightness so light it banished my cloud
and his gesture of ease spoke with a smile
"here now this is how life can be; like this:
light as the tippety-tap-tap of these old bones
and the merry-merry jig of a little tin whistle"

He was black and silver as a leprechaun
pink-skinned face a pastel dawn
his beard and hair a fine white mist
twirled down his waistcoat back
as his eyes rolled up underneath his hat
through his half closed lids I caught a glimpse
of the land where his music dwells

He called it forth to the bare-boarded room
in the pub where we stood that afternoon
"here now this is how" it sang to me
"life can be lived, like the tippety-tap-tap
of these two little bones
and the merry-merry jig of a whistle"

Gateways   1991

There are places that stop me to a sudden still
crossing of earth tracks on a woodland corner
echo of countless feet still press human warmth
upon a frosty landscape
time-corridor banked by hazel and beech root
against the wind-soaked hill

An olive grove where silence
sings bright as cicadas in the midday sun
and a tumult of ghostly whispers
beckon me to the threshing circle
centred hot red velvet
baked underfoot

Time past meets time present
on the treading of the stair
where a chorus waits
and river calls
where stone weeps
and tree watches

Savage Garden   2004

Underneath a cabbage leaf
lurks the hunter
between gentle fronds
of nigella
and heavy scented rose
death stalks
not just there
across the fence
in the combe
below the apple orchard
where buzzard swoops
fox prowls and badger digs
and our meat on the hoof still grazes

Right here
where nature
is tamed into
perennial swathes
ordered and clipped
forbidden from straying
beyond the border's edge
creatures are eating one another
on a daily basis

Savagery enters my house
a stoat
trapped on the stairs
on my
broadloom carpet
grade three for heavy domestic use
but was it designed
for slaughter?
its tiny fangs bared
in survival screams
pinned down

by my
fluffy feline friends
Beating off my cuddly companions
I try
heart thumping
to coax it
down and out
the door
unlike weasels
who know how to go pop!
it drags its bleeding body
among my shoes
smearing its life on my trainers
exhausted and rescued by dustpan
finally expired under
the lime green fronds
of alchemelia molis

On a daily basis
murder occurs
in God's little haven
where the righteous and retired
brandish their weapons of peace
the hoe and the hose
as snail is chewed
fly snapped
slug poisoned
frog squashed
mouse crunched
bird scooped
and badger hit
in the savage beauty
of the garden

Dusk 2004

It's luminous time
when cats
prowl
and lilac
glows
and vegetables
rest
from a hard day's
growing

It's luminous time
when rooks
stutter
and the zinc coal-hod
settles
against warm red brick
behind
the rhubarb

It's that brief spell
when day
contracts
to a magical tension
and colours
hypnotize
and blossom
hangs heavy
with fragrant mystery

spirit voices

She Who Walks With Stones And Sings   2004

Under a half-light canopy of silence
dappled pine-wood shade
the soles of her feet tread
moss cloaked grooves
of a forgotten other-world

"This is the place"
whispers the wind in branches
in her womb
her nether instincts tingle
as she gazes dreamily ahead
her spiral stick sinks into soft loam
following footprint memories
of the ancient way

In the gloom the gatekeeper rises
caught by shaft of speckled sun
a sandstone pillar chest-high
pitted and gnarled yet warm to touch
friends greet one another
as libation is poured
and prayers uttered
threading her way 'tween trunk and ditch
each stone sister reveals itself
some fallen, half buried in ferns
others still proud
all pleased to be found
and touched by loving heart and hand

Stroking their stone skin
she whispers their names
her breath on their surfaces
Child Maiden Mother Crone …
A circle of nine
nine dancing maidens

on the Mother - a hollow
filled with rain and grain
left by one who remembers

Singing softly at first
the stones fill her voice with feeling
until they ring out together
stirring the sleeping wood
into life and celebration
once more
"Give me a name dear sisters"
"Hshhh… Hasshhh…Hashaomi"…. they whisper
solemnly she asks its meaning
they sniff as if to say "what do *You* think?"
and "She who walks with stones and sings! "
retraces her steps back to this world
laughing with delight at her own folly

Hedge-witch 2004

Hedge-woman
witch-woman
which way?

Down byways
and sly ways
the old dirt track
losing herself
among leaves
and fallen acorns

A family with maps
pass by
led with gusto
by Father
whose aim is to get them
from a to – b to – c
her only aim is
to be and to see

She glances up vacantly
her mind already decayed
into leaf mould
and peaty brown puddles
moss and lichen clothe her limbs
and she
solid and gnarled
as oak overhanging
bright rushing water

Hedge-woman
witch-woman
rich woman
traces her dreams
along quiet streams
of hidden valleys
leaving the heady bracken heights
for those who need to get somewhere!

Inner Voices 1991

"Listen to your inner voice," they say
"you only have to tune in
to the still small voice
and all will be made clear.
Trust," they say
"it'll tell you what to do and which way to go."

But how do I know if that voice
is the voice of my conscience
my Higher Self guiding me
through paths of righteousness
to some pre-arranged destiny?

Is it merely the voice of wishful thinking
the rational mind
or self-persecution subtly disguised?
Is it some invisible spirit guide
from the other side
or simply a projection
of my own lofty and grandiose imagination
luring me into blind alleys and other addictive
follies?

It beats me I can tell you
and I've practised you know, I've been trained
straining my inner ear
learning to discriminate
read between the lines
of the host of whispers
and tell the false voice from true
yet still I find myself in spiritual pratfalls
let down confused and blocked by circumstance
apparently misread

"Ah well!
that's telling you something," they say

"probably the wrong time"
"but what!" I say
in exasperation
"is it telling me? -
You're just moving the goalposts"

You should try listening
inside my head for a change
and see if you can find God in there!

Pilgrimage 1986

The coachload groans reluctantly
as Cretan dawn breaks by the soft sea edge
instant zorba kills all slumber
with a clamour of canned bazouki
and we mount drowsy into the day

Endless ragged slopes we climb
littered with carob tree and thorn
hour after dusty hour
I really thought we'd missed it

O' the utter surprise of Lesithi!
fairyland plateau
pastured green and white with apple blossom
tucked in mountain peaks
a thousand cloth-eared windmills
pulse to the midday sun

Still we climb till we come to the place
gathering candles
we stretch sleepy limbs along the path
prayer floods my mind

Old mountain way veiled in mists
here I contemplate the past
for mine and not mine I journey to free my heart
from Mothers spoiled shall my true Mother see
the Goddess is here everywhere!

Old mountain way full of surprises
freedom wisdom and compassion I ask of thee

Freedom from all that has been and not been
freedom from hurts men and women have done me
freedom from the world and to be in it
from fear from loneliness
(words planted with each step)

Wisdom to know the right path
to use freedom well
wisdom to know the difference between freedom and desire
to grow from my mistakes
wisdom to teach those who desire freedom

Compassion for those who wrong me and those I wrong
compassion for myself and for life
I ask of thee

    here at the great cave of Dicti
      tiny votive flames
  descend
like a spiral of sparks
  into the yawning black of
     earth's
        womb
      nothing changes
    endless processions
of
       unknowing pilgrims
   still tread
the
  millennia
      down
          to pay You homage

deep inside a fold of rock
I snatch a moment before the crowd gathers
a voice whispers "Here you may place your offering"
one last glance at a marriage now defunct
hurriedly I place my ring in the crevice

the guide's voice booms in the darkness
"IN THIS CAVE ZEUS WAS BORN!"
and so am I!

Innana's Journey 2000

One foot on the step
is all it takes to change a life
while the other lingers
in warm ochre dust

A foot on the step
presses stone-chill knowledge
from sole to knee in an instant
of Chinese whispers

That's all it takes to the Great Below
neither cashmere shawls nor lapis beads
can retain your dignity

Memories of a lover's kiss
on the mezzanine
cannot warm you
chorus's of adulation
will not help you face this one down

Did I say face?
nothing quite prepares you
for the icy blast
of meeting your other half
in the dark mirror
obsidian eyes cut an ego to shreds
less than a maggot
on the flyblown arse of a decaying donkey
all you can do is rot
and pray for release

At last your heart opens to love
that unforgiving bitch of envy and rejection
who you once banished after all
till she reclaimed you
and you crawl back up to the light

thankful only for the grace of breath
your eyes deeper by three miles

"Now you are fit"
she whispers
"to call yourself Queen"

Signs   2004

"Look for the signs"
she said
the buzzard overhead
a bird in the hand
the lie of the land
a glimmer between
twilight trees
voice in your ear
a gift in your dreams
the look of a stranger
that catches your eye
a book that draws you
you don't know why

" These are the ways spirit speaks"
she said
" to a soul asleep
just follow the thread"
the veins of the planet
catch fire in your arm
the spell of a spider
the glint of a charm
follow the footprints
follow the way
if you feel lost
you stop and you pray
they may not answer
you have to go deep
to stir and awaken the soul asleep

This priestess of magic
her hair a bright blaze
her eyes the green ocean
so deep was her gaze
she made me believe

in a world full of meaning
that life is alive
it is we who are dreaming

For She is the weaver
and we are the web
our souls are connected
to life by Her threads

Proud 2000

An' when I am nothing
like a little los' child seed
waitin' in de dark belly
I go down to de sea
Yemaya eh! Yemaya eh!
Mother Ocean
help me!

An' she say,
"You woman you proud!
You woman you proud!
you is de sea
you is de rock
you is de grass
you is de tree!

Take me into your child place
into your belly
take me into your heart
an' let de sing come out!"

An' de wave she rise me
all de way up to my heart
an' me sing
" Me Woman me proud
me woman me proud
me proud, me proud, me proud!"

artist's eye

Corners - A Painting Project   1995

                    lines
                    rectangular
                    triangular
                    perpendicular
  meet in pre-ordained definition
(of course they do)
then   push perception
             until solid walls bend
             stonework expectations
collapse
                         fly
oooooOOOOOUT
              (why shouldn't they?)
          turn the corner
     of
my tunnel vision
into an abstract world
                     see afresh
without needing to draw   an arch
   or
the light beyond
                 evoke
        without explanation
the tunnel effect
no longer cornered
                     torn
cardboard
 any old
  newspaper
   plain dirt
    aesthetically placed
     red on ochre grey richness
     will do

Blocked   2004

With my head upon the block
blocked at every turn
I bash my head
my hands, my soul
to no avail
if only it'd go away
if only I could smash it!

Giving up at last
exhausted but unbroken
I stare at the wall ahead
devoid of any notion

After a countless while
curiosity creeps in
reaching out I clasp the block
touch it to cheek and lips
savour its woody smell
regard its perfect geometry.

Perambulating its perimeter
I view its other sides
comprehend its history
pierced by rusty nail
responding to its suffering
I take it to my heart
my block becomes poetry at last

Barbara Hepworth's Garden   2004

Peopled by stone
form and space to view the world
punctuating plant shapes
bronze and slate
through shafts of green bamboo
pierced by peace and birdsong
seagulls mew the distance
of light and wave
from tranquil shade
to pool and leaf

Her workshop
a symphony to shades of white
stone-dust overalls
hung in rows
her strength and fury
rests
among rows of rusting rasps
and iron hammers
laid out in surgical readiness
for a goddess' blacksmith hands
to hew
back into life

On this June day
a Mediterranean stillness
hovers
in sculptor's paradise corner
where stone and bronze carve
the eye of the looker
her ghost
lingers
between fingers of trees
hollows of stones
kisses
the curved surfaces
of her children

family patterns

Family Patterns   1996

Layers of culture clothe the memory
patterns cut, tailored to the individual
ready for the customer's return
for the next generation to grow into
with a few minor alterations
the magic suit is discarded at death
collected and disposed of by the bereaved
bearing labels of residential homes
the scent of their owner still clings
memories of childhood
the comfort of Mummy and Daddy
before they returned to an infant dotage
pockets that held threads
photos, hearing aid batteries
pens, documents, memories
permission to reside
identity

Like Mama Used to Make   1996

Recipes are my history book - my dissertation
Booba's recipe for borscht,
for blintzes
Ukranian borscht, not Polish like Mrs Malinski's
real Russian purple - is this a soup!
and this is how you make a knedlech,
a latke, a kreplach
My Mother's chopped liver wasn't as good as Rose's
but could she pickle a herring,
stuff a helzel, bake a honey cake
like air it would melt in your mouth
a real balabusta!
recipes - the heritage of women
prayers lovingly handed down,
mother to daughter
keeping body and soul of a tradition
alive and well in its identity

Absent   1993

"It must be very hard", she said
in that sympathetic tone people have
when they want you to know
that they really know
how you feel
but they don't
well she didn't anyway

And you know I was surprised
I still am
when I heard my voice say
"not really, I don't really care, I'm afraid"

How can one possibly say such a thing
about one's Mother?
without even a tinge
of the old familiar guilt

Meanwhile Mother sits vacant
vegetating in permanent care
unable to lift food to mouth
with fingers
shouldn't I care?

Part three they call it
as if dementia were the third and final
act of life
after the last commercial break

The truth is she vacated long ago
and this
the logical conclusion
all my life I grieved her absence
no need to pretend that she's there for me
no need to frustrate myself with guilt and rage
about not wanting to be there for her
relief that the show's over
now we can both rest in peace

Last Kaddish 1997

You left long ago
and now your body
free
regaining your memory
your speech your dancing
little russian girl
*Esfira

The rabbi intones
and I lead for the last time
"yitgadal v-yitkadash sh'may rabah"
now it's I who finds it hard to remember
your voice, your words, my Mummy
lost in eight years of disphasic fading
into see-through being
nothing left but your smile
which fills the chapel space above your coffin
beaming love to us all
gone the decades of rage and guilt pressed in
keeping our competing needs at telephone length
only love remains
and the shock of your sudden presence
jerk tears as I say
"chirutay v'yamlich malchutay
oseh shalom bimromav hu yah'ahsay shalom"
then who will say kaddish for me?

*Esfira (Esther)

K*lops* 1998

She made me klops
rich meatloaf, tomato-gravy
spiked with garlic
she gave me tsouris and spilkes
neuroses with my knadlech
shhhh don't rock the boat!
don't be too jewish!
was her hidden message
but oh the klops
and the borscht
fed my soul to qvelling

Three Course Meal   2004

Befores

Regular attendance was expected
not that he paid much attention
deaf to the world and Mother's demands
he'd perform remarkable vanishing acts
between " dinner's nearly ready"
and the quiet thump of plate on tablecloth

Starters

To be followed by a ritual of
"Where's Daddy gone now?"
and an exasperation of "Naaaat!"
commanding all corners of the house
but not his ears.
He'd be found opportunely washing his hair
or catching a convenient shuteye
(he invented the powernap)
eye's shielded by hankie - hearing aid off,
to be jolted awake
by an accompaniment of frustrated finger

Afters

Often his absence
returned his plate to the oven
only to be retrieved crisp and sepia at the edges
un-phased he ate up the long evening silence
sodden with war like an angry impending pudding

Mains

Mainly we sat
anticipating the awful moment
before a mouthful could be swallowed

and the demanding "Well?"
lurched our stomachs
draining any possibility of appreciation from our lips
rather provoking a desire to regurgitate
in stubborn rebellion against
the oven full of resentment served by my Mother

These were the dishes of my childhood.

Animus 1991

Mother's fears clutched me to her angry bosom
all those years preventing me from having you
jealous I might win your favour
yet quite oblivious of the fact

Such savage infant truths
that take us by the throat
in our struggle to survive
lie deep in shadow
kick bite and scratch
are replaced by subtle put-downs
and other domestic martyrdoms

I could tear her throat out for keeping me from you
paralysing the desire
and desperate the struggle to find you
in the dark land where I hid you

Now I've got you to myself
choosing to forget
how your self-pity left me marooned
too great my need to know that magical word
FATHER
a steady hand
the voice that says
"you can my daughter, you can do it"
watch me put my foot
out on the doorstep
of the big wide world
honour my difference
help me be proud of being a woman
teach me trusty friendship of man

Of course you weren't up to it
save for enough snatches here and there

to finish the job off myself
now my tender lame lover
reflects your pale moon face, passive and helpless
so it's time to take my leave Daddy dear
now I know my dark side
I can walk on at last
out of the moonshine swamp of tears
into the sunshine
where a strong golden man awaits me

Magic Suit   1995

They gave me his hearing aids today
these were my Father's ears
they gave me his eyes in a spectacle case
his clothes in a black bin bag
and the Rolex copy still ticking away his time on earth
when they handed me his credit cards I knew there'd be
                                                debts to clear

When they took me to see his body
I wanted to know
if they'd left his teeth in
I never saw him without his teeth
they offered me a sherry and I went in
two carnations on his chest
low hum of air conditioning
face smooth as the pillow
not a line nor a furrow left

I couldn't look at his hands under the quilt
elegant fingers that had fashioned and styled
"Southport tailor's magic suit" read the clippings
of which he'd kept countless copies
one jacket to fit all sizes was the claim
now its secret dies with him
I loved his hands and the crooked little finger
from the accident in Cornwall before I was born

At his funeral I wanted to play "I did it my way"
cause he certainly did driving us crazy in the process
so I touched his arm and said goodbye
"eighty-five not a bad innings" she said
and the nurse took the glass from my hand

Release   1995

Rocks stitched with french-knot pink
reel above a joyous sea
pennywort beads the crevices
as white froth swirls below
who says death is dark
or grief its doleful companion?
I tread cliff-tops under a bright sky
as paternal memories flutter over the edge
summoned by spiralling gulls

In the midst of the limitless sky
a buzzard hangs
in a sphere of light
a floater in God's eye.

The Golem   1994

If I knew I had no control over time
I'd have to/ I could
stop driving my frantic self
to have to get it all done NOW
to have to tell you everything NOW
to have to cram it all into NOW

If i don't i'll never get another chance
i don't know when i'll get another chance
time with you comes so rarely
i have to make you think i'm as special to you
as you are to me
so you'll stay even a few more minutes longer
i have to make you think i'm really special
to get what i want
like Heidi my cat butting her head under my hand
to get each stroke

those few precious minutes of yours
have to last months for me
moments of bright sanity
in the home of the blind and deaf

if I knew I had no control over seeing
then I'd have to/I could
choose to come off guard duty
because someone has to see in the dark
everyone else is blundering around
bumping into each other treading on each other
and thinking it normal
and because they're older than me
i'm supposed to obey them

if I knew I had no control over knowing
I'd have to/I could

let go of needing to keep the light on
desperately searching for
juggling through and pointing out all possible answers
i could stop holding up the world
our world, your world, mine

I'd have to find a new definition of special
I'd have to replace glamour with the real thing
I'd have to let myself and others be
I'd have to let go and let love
I'd be free to create and mind my own business
I'd have to dismantle the golem.

Glamourseekers   1994

Glamour is special
glamour is scarce
glamour is seeking special as scarce
like those too few precious moments when
Mummy really listened to what you had to say
when you really felt she understood what you meant

like when teacher picked you out
and you felt shiny all over

glamour is time
so rare between
shopping and cooking and "Can't stop now dear
I'm BUSY!"

when you wanted to share the magic
of watching a snail's eyes unfold

No time between "Daddy's home!"
and "Bed!"
no space between rows that lasted
from the coming in until the going out
harsh voices pierce the magic
like fog on the brain like knife in the heart
shrinking into a safe invisible corner

later perhaps
once in a blue moon
the magic returns

Big sister in a sticky-out ball gown
earrings shaped like pagodas
glides into the darkened room
home for Christmas holiday
taffeta whispers and Chanel number five wake the senses

"Sorry darling I thought you were asleep"
"it's alright did you have a nice time?"
"yes shhh! go back to sleep"

a moment with Daddy when
he sits with you in the shadows
watching shadows dance in the twilight
together

Together the magic is safe
alone the shadows loom
glamour is special
glamour is scarce
glamour is selling special as scarce
and it's big business granting favours
to those who think they can't afford
to miss being one of the chosen few
too used to chasing the longing
to know the real thing
gurus, divas, showmen
purveyors of longing, masters of special

it takes a hungry child
to make a master of special

Sisters 1987

Friendship is about trying and not trying
friendship is about saying "bullshit" when they're lying
friendship is also about dying

Who'd have thought that the deepest love I'd ever share
would be with you my sister
but when I look in my heart the tender pain of love
still catches my breath with a gasp

all my life I reached out for you but my fingers
clutched the air
you weren't where I expected you to be

You cared I cared
but our language for the world was different
you with your Estee Lauder perfume
Conservative lunches and Harrods account
me with my downtrodden bohemian ways
and the dope
the chip-on-the-shoulder dreamy little sister

then cancer
it was your birth-sign
it was your death-sign too

Holding your hand, soothing your tears
witnessing your torment
bathing your shrinking body
were some of the most precious moments of my life
I'll never forget sitting hand in hand
one sunny afternoon
silently sharing love by your bedside
soul gazed into soul as eyes met
and you said
"it looks like the sun's coming out of your face"
now I've lost you to another place

I'm proud of what we shared
Diana you were magnificent in your dying
no smallness at all
and me the larger for having been there for you
and for me of course
but that's friendship

Memoriam   2004

Mostly I remember your voice
your turn of phrase
slender grace of your arms
so unlike my solid branches
you the dancer /singer
me the artist/ actress
you could be silly and fun to laugh with
when you weren't being sensible older sister
which was most of the time
you were the unflappable centre-post
leaving us all in your perfect shade

But there was a price to pay
your emotional rigidity
your unbending rationality
always demanding "But how do you know?"
when the answer was,
"I just feel it!"

Like the hexagram "splitting apart"
the post collapsed
and we scattered
Mother to Alzheimer's
Father and son-in-law
to endless co-dependent wrangling
Daughter to hide
behind dependable controlling man
Son to clam like rage
and I?
forced to grow up at last
find my feet, clip my wings
join the adult world
instead of raiding your fridge
perching cuckoo like upon your sofa
escaping parental dysfunction

It's years since you went
and we survived somehow without you
but our lives indelibly stained
by the loss of you

Thankful to Trees   1998
(of Putney Heath)

It's a strange occupation
waiting for death
three times I waited while
finger branches soothed
breathing my aura clean
solidity of oak and beech rooted me
in the suspension of hours

Taking a breather from
my sister's endless winding down
sobbing "Amazing Grace" to the great beech while
a squirrel raced

Planting a sapling of ash over
Father's ashes
the resident's association refused
to let me put it in the garden
said they'd prefer a bench so
I placed it outside the gate instead
clawing badger-like in the undergrowth

Mother's spirit danced free
through the broad oak heath
promise of eternity
glinting gold between the green
and the satisfying crackle
of dried husk underfoot

Round Barrows   1995

Two myrtle mounds crouch cat-like
in the oilseed
a sudden sea of chrome
guarding the once sacred land
where iron bones from ochre burnt
are returned to ancestral loam
the citrus acre sings out
unashamed as a suburban parlour in the midday sun

Yellow is our rape of the earth
and Vincent's last blazing look at a cornfield world
against the black fleeing crows
over the Mendip horizon a viridian fringe of trees
swish like a crematorium backdrop

Only a week later, cut down by the lammas scythe
my Mother's dead jaw hangs slack
in a green/yellow field of a face
far from where the Russian steppes of her birth
billow golden with wheat

now, olev hashalom
both parents lie scattered on foreign soil
while its original occupants are exiled under margarine
yitgadal v'yitkadash shmey rabah
for all our ancestors
sing unashamedly yellow in the midday sun!

love poems

Invitation   1992

How would you like to
slip into something special with me?
fingertips brushing eyelashes
heart to heart

then nearness and solid as tree-trunks
growing side by side
rough bark cracking
eventually into interesting shapes

how would you like to
slip into moistness
of soft sea petals
undulating passion

O' do say yes!

Aflame 2000

You bore holes in my heart
to the core of my being
twenty five miles deep
to molten rock
I'm aflame with your touch
our bodies caress express
the passion the joy
but can they really articulate
is it really only a week?

Lady Of The Lake 2000

You are my lake
that I will swim in
sink in
rising from weed beds
silt in my mouth
break surface
float in satin ripples
ears ringing
as I gulp in this
pure moment of life

Pierced by Excalibur's
radiant blade
fish-mouth flaps
as I dive again
to taste the depths of you

Love Hits   2000

Love hits
amazed
as phosphorus at
the gaping
hole in my chest

Love weds
me   to
the   wind
to music
the dead   hare
by the roadside

Old perceptions
slip   like
 a
  tv
        pic
          ture

The unending journey
over
the   ghost   train
has arrived
on   time
spilling me   out
onto
the platform   at
your feet

Storm In A Teacup   2004

I stalked the road that night
glancing through windows
at other fire-lit lives
were the tvs laughing
their calculated laugh at me?
faces washed in sodium yellow guilt
passed on the other side
and testosterone roar of fiesta
shook my paranoia
as it shot by

My anxiety too big to contain
paced the block
over and over
what I said what you said
what I thought you said but didn't say
what I didn't say but wished I had
but the houses were indifferent
the moon clouded
and the world an unsprung trap
set for me alone
desperately I tried to claw back control
to find and put
the safety catch back on

Where was it? what was it this time?
was it over between us?
was this just another
storm in a teacup?
I looked up
saw the tiny light slowly crossing
its arc across the great
black, blue black heavens
in a moment of wonder
the storm was over.

Swan Song   2004

"And so you bloody should!"
her voice, a savage force
a dark mirror juxtaposed
against memories of passion
fragments of milky intimacy

She stands
I sit
she at the door
I in the middle of the floor
where once was lushness and ease
a dry stone river-bed carves the room
between us

Through cracks of thorny accusation
a rivulet of recall
tendrils of familiar longing
reach across the ravine
gaining honeysuckle holds
on our startled flesh
soothing re-stimulating
until our bodies
do what they know best
and flesh
collapses into flesh

O' the relief of familiar softness
of warm silky breath and holding
of nestling between
of moulding well remembered shapes
into practised folding
and fingers urgently tunnel
back to that haven we made
since lost in the tangle
of who said what
and did, or failed to do which
to whom

The sharpness of it all
dissolves with her cry
then a tide
of relief ebbs
into a quiet nestling
each in the other's bosom
deep into the night
by firelight
cradling each the other
with favourite tendernesses

"I know you," she said
a fatal remark
"I know you love me more than her
and you always will."

Not any more
and a thorn reappears
then others
and there it is
the unassailable desert and the longing
side by side forevermore

And we sigh
the sigh of surrender
so small so final
our chilled bodies request clothing
and retrieving scattered knickers, socks
once gifted and washed by
the others' hands
become the raiment of strangers
with only wool to replace her arms about me
silently we retrace our steps
leaving our lips on the coffee cups by the hearth
and an abandoned tee-shirt behind the sofa

Hostage   1994

There's something so seductive
about her hurt
the feeling of compassionate anguish
is quite exquisite
it seems only reasonable
to want to ease her heart with mine

Beneath there…
lies
a need
that won't be fixed
and so becomes
the drama of endless
suffering and blame
gasping for breath
but never expired
catching us all
in its appalling thrall
of fury

So well constructed
through years of repetition
and knife-sharp brain
that the seam cannot be found
let a lone argued

Despite knowing this
and guarding the moment when
I might tumble in
it's only ever after
I realise
hook line and sinker
yet again I fell

Harvest At St Ives 2000

Silver ribbons the creamy sand
as we, on the edge
of parting
staying
ebb and flow
releasing fears, projections
endeavouring with grace
without rancour
to accept our differences

Mother Ocean's steady flow
nudges at Pandora's box
bobbing before us
and the hope
that we still can
remains

A giant golden plate moon
glides slowly up
into a gentle sky

It is not a harsh edge
the moment is true
is beautiful
the loss real
that we have no power
or right to control

At last I surrender
to this soft sand
not knowing
freeing you and I

The moon now shrunk
to its familiar silvered form
rainbow halo
sharp and clear

Surrender 2004

When was it I realised
my fears for the future
were truth?

How many years spent bruising knuckles
against an unassailable fate
before failure became acceptance?

No longer railing
against the heap of broken hearts
loneliness became grace

Giving up isn't so bad
when you can't win
just stopping the battle
brings rest and simple gratitude

My friend apologised at the checkout
for only buying for one
"I'm not really alone"
she said
"He's away for the weekend,
the kids are with their Father!"

I spent most of a life alone
but I'm no longer apologising
just glad to be here
and loved
by friends
growing old
with cats
and a good book.

mending the broken self

Beneath 2000

Beneath untouchedness
is touch
is grieving
beneath a blanket of forgetting
joy still breathes

Beneath cold
is blood
is rage
warm river
beneath the carapace of ice
a tender heart still flows

Behind cynicism
is fear
is betrayal
is curiosity
behind a steel door
wonder and innocence still play

And when
life breathes
and heart flows
and wonder plays again
the frozen broken child
becomes at last the woman

Need   1994

"Empty as a pocket" Paul Simon says
pocket seems safe
snug
something to snuggle into
be carried in

empty as...
quick! shut-it-out
put-the-kettle on-
grab-a-biscuit-stuff-it-down
clean-the-kitchen-the windows-the taps
avoid the void

empty as...
a desert
pick-up-the-phone-who-can-i-phone?
who-else-can-i-phone?
who-can-i-tell-ephone?
"hi! what-are-you-up-to?
never-mind-another-time-bye!"

an aching desert
screaming from neck to groin
stuff-it-with-people-things-tv-quick
before-it-gobbles-the-planet
a pocket-a pocket
a hammock to swing me
soothe me
hold me
fold me
rock me
in my cradle
safe and sound
till i can let
go to solid ground

Fences 1996

"After all it's not the crime of the century"
I said to Carol as she scooped up George's
protesting body into his chair
"sounds like over-reaction" she said
memories of my neighbour bearing down on me
her anger before her like bull-bars
when I tore down the fence

It's time to set new bounds
no longer walled in shame
while accusers on both sides of the fence toss blame
to be free to love we must be free to reject
the toddler's right to declare
I hate you Mummy I don't love you any more!
sever the bonds of birth
but my crime lay unuttered hostage to maternal frailty
and ranks of paranoid lovers
whose arsenal of accusations
could not break the spell
I put on my mouth

Now the fences are down
replaced by palisades
interspersed with gaps for light and flowers to twine
around my heart
finally I'm ready for love cause after all
it wasn't the crime of the century

New Year Resolution   1997

Sniff the track, catch the scent
poke snout out of burrow into sharp frosty air
as the echoes of the last departing guest subside
and in the quiet of these first days
I wonder where the wind'll blow me

Letting go, learning to disentangle
are the seeds my soul picked out for me to cultivate
from this new century's catalogue.

Sinking snout into wet leaf mould
of the little earthy track
I determine to follow through hazel thickets
to Vobster and beyond
savouring the new sensation
of departing from obsess and possess
and other mind-fields of intensity.

Leaving the self-accuser at the crossroads
her baggage of blame now redundant about her feet
her sharp finger-nose will gather dewdrops instead
and me no longer there for her to point at

If we could learn
to leave our hate at the threshold;
if we could do this
what a pile there'd be
what a World!

There Comes A Time   2000

There comes a time when
it's time to stop
the roaring
in your ears
fierce tide
smashing against
the rocks of your heart

You stop
the sound stops
waves grow into
calm lapping rhythms
and the thought
that just a moment before
you were nearly drowning
seems strange

The massive head
and muzzle
of the white bull lowers
and bobs
sniffing my fingers
pushes his giant inquisitive eyes
into my face
searching for the slightest sign
but there was none
just this once
and that's when
the time came to stop
being afraid

Heart Of Darkness 1998

Sometime between
breakfast and
the lunchtime post
I slipped
through a wormhole
finding myself
or some semblance
back nowhere
in that other universe

and in the
terrifying empty
deep black dark
that goes on and on and on and on
in all directions forever
i cannot see

i got left behind
they forgot i existed
so i'm not sure if i do
except the pain that scrapes
the inside of my skin
with a howl as big as a mountain

and in the centre was
is
a tiny
spark that
defies the dark
and is warm
and is whole
and is love
and i decided i could
fill myself with it
and i did

until it became
the whole universe
and out I popped
joyous to the letters
on the mat

Healing   1996

There's the healing of telephone calls
you, there
at the end of my line
the comfort of voice
of Radio Four
in the long night

There's the empowerment of wren
russet blur flashing into thickets
Its bold clack proclaiming
"take heart! take heart! "

There's the simplicity of walking
step by step down though the hell
of mind obsession
to a muddy, prickly
grassy, luscious
sharp-scented stillness
of body-being
and limbs
that are pleased to bend.

There's the song of streams
the generosity of trees
patience of stone
and sweetness of air
on sallow, jaded flesh

There's healing everywhere
in a rejoicing of birds
the cleansing of sea
the tolerance of bees
and kindness of earth
that receives and turns loss
into beauty and birth

Survivor's Sunset   2004

You speak your poem
the first time
aloud
your back to
the window

As you unpeel your memory
of unspeakable
betrayal
I gaze over your shoulder
to a sky
all glory of crimson and gold

Recounting your toddler's guidebook
to incest survival
a triumph
of invention
while the new moon
like a nail paring
twins Venus rising

The Client   2004

Sullen you sit
opposite
the gap between our chairs
three miles

"Help me" you say
while your eyes defy anyone
to reach your heart
to relinquish your pain -
the ultimate betrayal

Who was it exactly
thought it'd be
a good idea for you to come
partner, colleague, family friend?
all rendered powerless
to cure you

Their love lies
like crumpled underwear
round your feet
so they pass you to me
their frustrated pleas
pinned to your chest
"Please help this person
we're at wits end!"

Already I sense
the tug of rescue
and certain knowledge of defeat

Sidestepping
I wait and try
to see it from your chair
praise your determination

admire the suffering which defines you
your most precious possession
now we're ready
to begin the session.

No More 2000

All my life
I've been forced to fit where I don't
fit scissors, pens, cake-forks
and cheque books
in a right-handed world
sinisterly

Carrying the Lilith thing
the Jewish thing
the lesbian thing
the rogue and vagabond
thespian thing
exposed invisible psychic creative thing

I was the unheard
the unseen
unacceptable inexplicable threat
who wanted only to belong

I learned your language
tried to be nice
remembering not to ring
at five o' clock or ten- to- three
we the childless have to know these details
remembering always to ask
"How are the children?
You must be proud"
and "that must be hard for you"
lose your company at half-term

When did you ever learn my language?
When did you ever consider the need?

All my life, all my life
I learned the script

the responses
the gestures
the look
but was there ever really any point
I was despite it all different

Now I stand in my own right
have learned to face the pain
own the rage
release the cynical humour
forgive and let go
made a bag of wisdom with it all
embroidered with magical hare and swan
and the exquisite cup of love I found
having filled it first with myself

Now I stand in my own light
and watch as the world comes to me
letting it pass by
welcoming those who want to stop and honour me

My spirit soars
for this is the time of the outsider
now the outside is in
and the inside fades
to a better proportion
we're coming, we're here
as we always have been
the veil is off at last
watch out!

When Life Feels Blue   2003

When life feels blue
just say, "POOH!"
and don't let the bastards get you

Wear lots of pink
have forty winks
or wanks if that's what helps you

Plant some seeds
string some beads
and with every one say "Bless you"

Paint your room
take a broom
and clear out all that stops you

Feel free to chant
buy a plant
anything that suits you

Plot vengeance schemes
have fabulous dreams
anything that tells you

You're the best
and they're the worst
just don't let the BASTARDS GET YOU!

all-sorts

Threshold   2004

That moment when
hand on cool glass door
heart pounds
anticipating when
heads now bowed
in chatter over latte
will raise
and stop
turn
and stare
hinges will sound
when I push
a café full of eyes will glare
and whisper "It's her!"
sweep me from head to foot
devouring every detail

Am I in the right gear?
I should've worn my other jacket
Is my hair ok? I knew I should have washed it
I'm sure my eye make-up's smeared
my lippy's out of date
will they notice my new bag?
Does my bum stick out? My legs too fat?

O that excruciating moment!
how I wish I could hide up my sleeves
my face behind my hair
curl up by the tv 'til it's over
and I'm a woman
like my Mum
well not like her
but you know what I mean
old and sagging and couldn't care less
if boys rate her
or friends approve

O shit!
here goes
whatever you do just look cool
"Hya gang! how's it going?
Mine's a latte - got a fag?"

Ladies of a Certain Age   1995

They used to meet on the third floor of department stores
in nameless seaside towns
swapping gossip and ailments in low innuendo
across the napery
stirring potions in teapots, powdering away blushes
drawing comfort from teacakes
after the surgical nip and tuck
while the gliding models paused to display
the latest in casual daywear

Now the burn-your-bra generation has come of age
rewriting midlife and celebrating croneage
now it's support groups and HRT, or women against HRT
and that herbal cream you get from Ireland
to fan the flames of a vanishing libido
douse the rose-madder furnace rushing up your throat
exercising pelvic floor muscles when the knicker-elastic's gone
in your genitals and you've forgotten why
"now where was I...? sorry I've gone spaghetti- brained again"
gets a laugh these days
and ageism demands your full dedication
libido and stamina enhancement supplimentation
step aerobics, ginseng sandwiches and wild yam risotto for tea
fifty-five and still runs ten orgasms round the block
before the executive board meeting

But mourning still lingers in the silence
too late for children now
too late for any more
when aging and saging doesn't seem quite so attractive
when a spreading waist and the feeling
of being dragged to a downhill future
withdraws you into a bow-headed wisdom of acceptance
as the body takes its toll against the wishes of the mind

Senior Moment   2004

I'm having a moment
a senior moment
a mentalpause
I'm so very peri-mentalpausal
or Perry Como as my friend calls it

Each time I think; this could be a poem
it evaporates distracted by some other
thing, thought, sight,
or suddenly remembered task
and days go by
every so often it drifts back into consciousness
like delicious wood-smoke promising pleasure
Ah yes! I must do it I must compose a....
I could write a ......
I could write a ......
a ..... a ...
Fuck! what's the word?
something to do with dancing
Latin American tango
no!
dango, fandango no!
danza yes! biodanza
shit! what's the word?
why won't it leap out of the back of my head like it used to?
astound me with verbal agility
springing delights from the filing cabinet of the cerebellum
or which ever part does it
that's it yes! stanza! I could write a stanza!

O' the humiliation of saying "grapefruit"
when you mean to say "bathroom"
"throat" when you meant "thrush"
having to resort to, "those round things in vinegar"
when the word "pickle" eludes you

it's scary
am I going to end up like Mother
on the Alzheimer mezzanine to eternity?
Lingering in wing-backed armchairs

The awful thing is I decide, on reflection
interspersed by conversations with various friends,
the awful answer to the question my friend asked me
the one "How do you know you are you?"
when I examine this when I really think it through
there's only one answer in the end
I know I am me through my memory,
it's my memory that tells me I'm me!

Sanction 1996

They sell them now in Sainsbury's
between the rice cakes and Ryvitas
low calorie yeast free
appealing to an eco-clientele
ever grazing nouveau pastures
ignorant of history
Rakusen's Matzot still bear the sanction of Beth Din

The Jew in me who craves acceptance
is pleased to share her special soulfood and smiles
deeper down another rankles
the wounded Jew cries out, "but this is mine sacred!"
Passover bread baked in memory of endless hurried
                                            departures
escape from the Angel of Death
no time to taste the yeast of life between slavery and desert
this precious freedom to be different so painfully won
is eaten once a year
how dare you take it from me!
would you wrap communion wafers in cellophane
and sell them too?

Jews were murdered for making matzot
not martyred blood of Christian boys
Little Hugh of Lincoln's voice resounds
with hundred's slaughtered in his name

Now they lie amongst slimming breads
while the gentle voice of irony intercedes
smiling at the thought the dead might
call this testimony to success instead
a place on the shelf; the final integration?

Miriam's Gift 1993

I have no menorah to give you
no candlesticks or lokshen soup
no centuries of suffering and sayings
no volumes of shoulds and shall nots
only this hot desert air and the simple peace of an oasis

While my brother waves his stick about
impressing everybody
turning truths into indisputable facts
I sing in a temple of endless sky
and dance my journey without end
to a land I see in my dreams
this is what it means to be Jewish!

Small Wonder   2004

Small wonder we fail
to comprehend utterly
the cruelty of war
the indifference to consequences
of global cartels
to suffering of strangers
when mostly
our broken hearts
and sadly sometimes limbs
are caused by those we know
and love

What of our own cruelty?
how many astound ourselves
with a sudden lashing out
that unthinking act
that flattens another's ego?

And if not others
what private acts of abuse
occur inside our heads?
daily beatings, shamings
"useless, pathetic, you'll never...."
small wonder!

The Last Lines   2004

(Inspired by the last lines of "Tall" by Carol Ann Duffy)

Who was there when they came
when the cattle trucks rattled through hell's gateway?
"work makes us free" the devil-workers cried
while the chimneys cast their unspeakable shadow
over a stained land

What mother could bear to watch over her children
on the short downward slope to their final solution
all the other gods had fled
and Yaweh Himself tried and found guilty
in His absence
one black Sabbath eve

Only one whose fury
could match this terrible place
her owl claws gripped the ashen ground
as she howled injustice
at the crackle of bone in greedy ovens
and rotting corpses heaped in pits

"I knew from the start"
she screamed to the darkened wind
"How he'd turn out to be, this Adam!"
"Yaweh you were a fool; a lousy Father!" she yelled
"and I'd have no truck with it!"
turning her tearstained face to the sky
Lilith spread her wings
embraced her children with tenderness
"and caught their souls in her hands
as they fell from the burning towers"

Islets Of Langerhan 2004

(a diabetic lament)

Paint me a sky
rose and gold
exotic paradise with sleepy lagoon
cry of parakeet winging over treetops
on steamy mountain slopes

I dream of a sweet archipelago
where honey blossom drowns the senses
and chocolate pools are fringed with meringue

But these mysterious isles
remain forever out of reach
a horizon fantasy
for this small vessel is becalmed
as a sugary undertow
crystallises the bows
and I starve in a sea of plenty

Dirty Beast   2004

Grubby knees
lick-spittle hankie
"Hold out your hands!"
Mother commands
"Now look at me!
The other way!"
erasing vanilla lipped pleasure
with rough determined scrubs

A mother's duty entails
continued removal of dirt
in all its varieties
dust from skirting board
grease from plate
tea from cup and tablecloth
lime-scale from kettle
earth under nail
berry juice of all types
and other droolings, leakages and slops
from skirt-front shirt-front
shirt-tail
biological residues and personal stains
from gusset
fluff from pocket
eliminate eliminations
scum and plimsoll line
from bathroom
bogey from nostril
vomit from lavatory bowl

A mother's constant battle
is to stamp out germs
banish the dirty beast in us
and cleanse us back to godliness
"Dirty beast - you dirty beast -
get out you dirty beast!"

Full Circle 2004

That's what it's like in the company of women
coming upon the trio of friends
straightway they fold me into their midst
snug as a hospital corner
melting into familiar
quintessentials of life
such as bathroom details
no longer competing for lovers
or fretting over childcare
like rooks cackling and crowing
seeking noisy solace over body-signs of ageing
settling those small but vital anxieties
"is it normal or is it me?"
no longer needing to shave a leg
pluck a chin instead
(razors move upwards with the years)
memory lapses and defiance against the clock

"She's always loved gadgets", explains Jane
while Lou obsessively fingers her wap phone
showing me a video of lambs she's fostered
one wrapped in her daughter's red jacket
for extra warmth
while new technology preserves the mothering instinct
her daughter's commentary rings out
"I came from my Mummy's vagina you know!"
heads turn from the next table in disbelief
while we fall about laughing
full circle!
but that's how it is with women!

Index of First Lines

A heron's steady gaze 18
After all it's not the crime of the century 81
All my life 90
An' when I am nothing 38
And so you bloody should! 72
Beneath untouchedness 79
Empty as a pocket Paul Simon says 80
Friendship is about trying and not trying 60
Geese fill a flat sky 14
Glamour is special 58
Great swathes of slate arch 16
Grubby knees 105
He raised the bone slivers to scoop up my soul 20
Hedge-woman 29
How would you like to 67
I have no menorah to give you 101
I stalked the road that night 71
I'm having a moment 98
If I knew I had no control over time 56
It must be very hard, she said 47
It takes something the size of a mountain 17
It's a strange occupation 64
It's luminous time 24
Layers of culture clothe the memory 45
Lines 41
Listen to your inner voice, they say 30
Look for the signs 36
Love hits 70
Mostly I remember your voice 62
Mother's fears clutched me to her angry bosom 52
On the bone edge 12
On the path, a man lies buried 15
One foot on the step 34
Paint me a sky 104
Peopled by stone 43

Recipes are my history book - my dissertation 46
Regular attendance was expected 50
Rocks stitched with french-knot pink 55
She made me klops 49
Silver ribbons the creamy sand 75
Small wonder we fail 102
Sniff the track, catch the scent 82
Sometime between 84
Sullen you sit 88
Swallows perch on telegraph wires 19
That moment when 95
That's what it's like in the company of women 106
The coachload groans reluctantly 32
There are places that stop me to a sudden still 21
There comes a time when 83
There's something so seductive 74
There's the healing of telephone calls 86
They gave me his hearing aids today 54
They sell them now in Sainsbury's 100
They used to meet on the third floor of department stores 97
Two myrtle mounds crouch cat-like 65
Under a half-light canopy of silence 27
Underneath a cabbage leaf 22
Walking the brown of Your earth into stiff limbs 13
When life feels blue 92
When was it I realised 76
Who was there when they came 103
Winter joy 11
With my head upon the block 42
You are my lake 69
You bore holes in my heart 68
You called in whispers 9
You left long ago 48
You speak your poem 87

PS AVALON PUBLISHING

About PS Avalon

PS Avalon Publishing is an independent and committed publisher offering a complete publishing service, including editorial, manuscript preparation, printing, promotion, marketing and distribution.
As a small publisher enabled to take full advantage of the latest technological advances, PS Avalon Publishing can offer an alternative route for aspiring authors working in our particular fields of interest.

As well as publishing, we offer a comprehensive education programme including courses, seminars, group retreats, and other opportunities for personal and spiritual growth. Whilst the nature of our work means we engage with people from all around the world, we are based in Glastonbury which is in the West Country of England.

new poetry books

Our purpose is to bring you the best new poetry with a psychospiritual content. Our intent is to make poetry relevant again, offering work that is contemplative and inspirational, with a dark, challenging edge.

self development books

We publish inspiring reading material aimed at enhancing your life development without overburdening you with too many words. Everything is kept as simple and as accessible as possible.

journals

With its full colour design, easy on-line availability, and most of all with its exciting and inspiring contents, *The Synthesist* journal is a popular offering to the psychospiritual world and beyond.

PS AVALON PUBLISHING
*Box 1865, Glastonbury,
Somerset BA6 8YR, U.K.*

www.psavalon.com

info@psavalon.com

Printed in the United Kingdom
by Lightning Source UK Ltd.
108361UKS00001B/166-213